Groundwater Restoration at Uranium In-Situ Recovery Mines, South Texas Coastal Plain

By Susan Hall

Open-File Report 2009–1143

U.S. Department of the Interior
U.S. Geological Survey

U.S. Department of the Interior
KEN SALAZAR, Secretary

U.S. Geological Survey
Suzette M. Kimball, Acting Director

U.S. Geological Survey, Reston, Virginia: 2009

For product and ordering information:
World Wide Web: http://www.usgs.gov/pubprod
Telephone: 1-888-ASK-USGS

For more information on the USGS—the Federal source for science about the Earth,
its natural and living resources, natural hazards, and the environment:
World Wide Web: http://www.usgs.gov
Telephone: 1-888-ASK-USGS

Suggested citation:
Hall, Susan, 2009, Groundwater restoration at uranium in-situ recovery mines, south
Texas coastal plain: U.S. Geological Survey Open-File Report 2009–1143, 32 p.

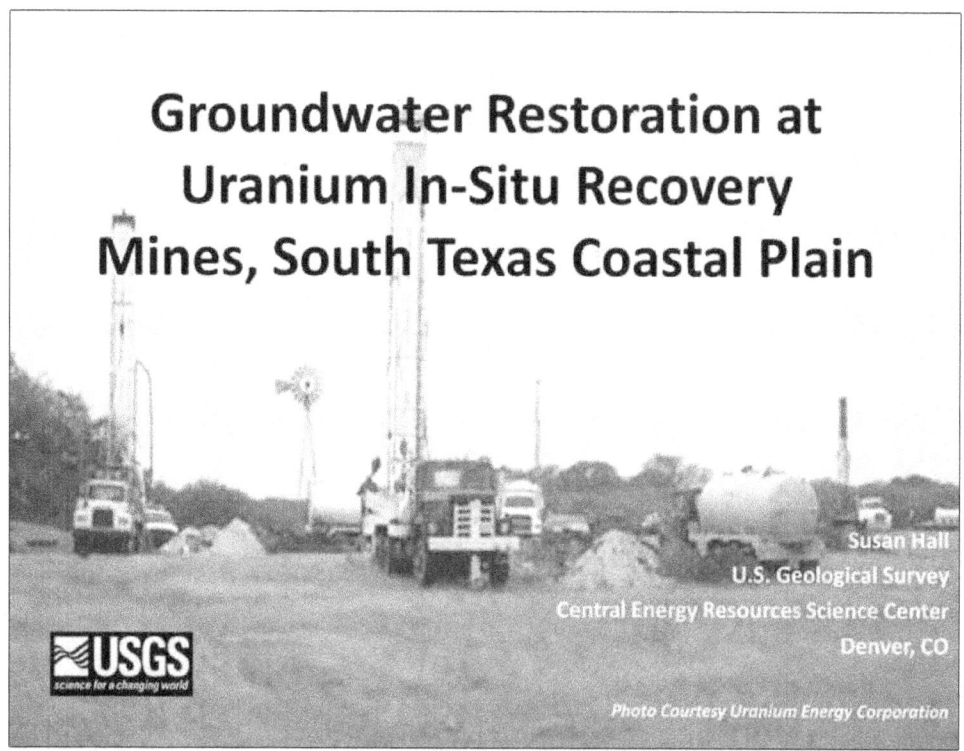

Groundwater Restoration at Uranium In-Situ Recovery Mines, South Texas Coastal Plain

Susan Hall
U.S. Geological Survey
Central Energy Resources Science Center
Denver, CO

Photo Courtesy Uranium Energy Corporation

Introduction

This talk was presented by U.S. Geological Survey (USGS) geologist Susan Hall on May 11, 2009, at the Uranium 2009 conference in Keystone, Colorado, and on May 12, 2009, as part of an underground injection control track presentation at the Texas Commission on Environmental Quality (TCEQ) Environmental Trade Fair and Conference in Austin, Texas.

Texas has been the location of the greatest number of uranium in-situ recovery (ISR) mines in the United States and was the incubator for the development of alkaline leach technology in this country. For that reason, the author chose to focus on the effectiveness of restoration at ISR mines by examining legacy mines developed in Texas. The best source for accurate information about restoration at Texas ISR mines is housed at the TCEQ offices in Austin. The bulk of this research is an analysis of those records.

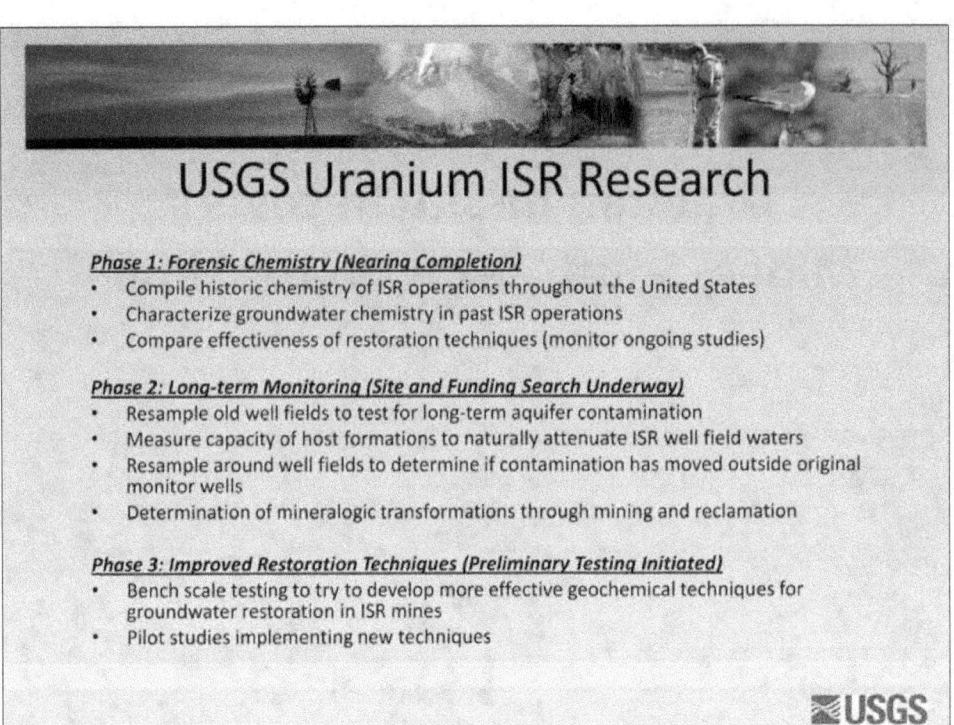

USGS Uranium ISR Research

Phase 1: Forensic Chemistry (Nearing Completion)
- Compile historic chemistry of ISR operations throughout the United States
- Characterize groundwater chemistry in past ISR operations
- Compare effectiveness of restoration techniques (monitor ongoing studies)

Phase 2: Long-term Monitoring (Site and Funding Search Underway)
- Resample old well fields to test for long-term aquifer contamination
- Measure capacity of host formations to naturally attenuate ISR well field waters
- Resample around well fields to determine if contamination has moved outside original monitor wells
- Determination of mineralogic transformations through mining and reclamation

Phase 3: Improved Restoration Techniques (Preliminary Testing Initiated)
- Bench scale testing to try to develop more effective geochemical techniques for groundwater restoration in ISR mines
- Pilot studies implementing new techniques

USGS Uranium ISR Studies

The USGS initiated a study of the effects on groundwater by ISR mining in 2008 in response to increased activity in uranium exploration and mining and the increasing number of applications for ISR mines to the U.S. Nuclear Regulatory Commission. USGS geologists were particularly intrigued with the widespread assertion that "Groundwater has never been returned to baseline at any ISR mine."

USGS ISR studies are broken down into three phases:

1. Compilation of forensic chemistry: the examination of legacy projects.
2. Investigations of groundwater chemistry over time.
3. Development of improved restoration techniques.

The USGS is nearing completion of Phase 1, the forensic chemistry portion of our project, and these are some of the interim results of this work. The search for a suitable field site and funding to evaluate long-term impacts and natural attenuation of groundwater in ISR well fields (Phase 2) is underway, and preliminary testing of new restoration technologies for ISR well fields (Phase 3) has begun.

Has Groundwater Been Restored
to Baseline at
Uranium In-Situ Recovery Mines
S. Texas Coastal Plain?

- Establishment of Baseline/Restoration Goals
- Effectiveness of Groundwater Restoration
- Long-term Stability and Natural Attenuation
- Best Restoration Technologies

Outline of Presentation

To determine the effectiveness of groundwater restoration at ISR mines, the following topics will be addressed:

1. The establishment of baseline and restoration goals.

2. Effectiveness of groundwater restoration.

3. Long-term stability of well fields.

4. An evaluation of best restoration technologies, including:
   (a) Pump and treat techniques (Texas),
   (b) The addition of reductants (Wyoming and New Mexico), and
   (c) Bioremediation (Nebraska and Wyoming).

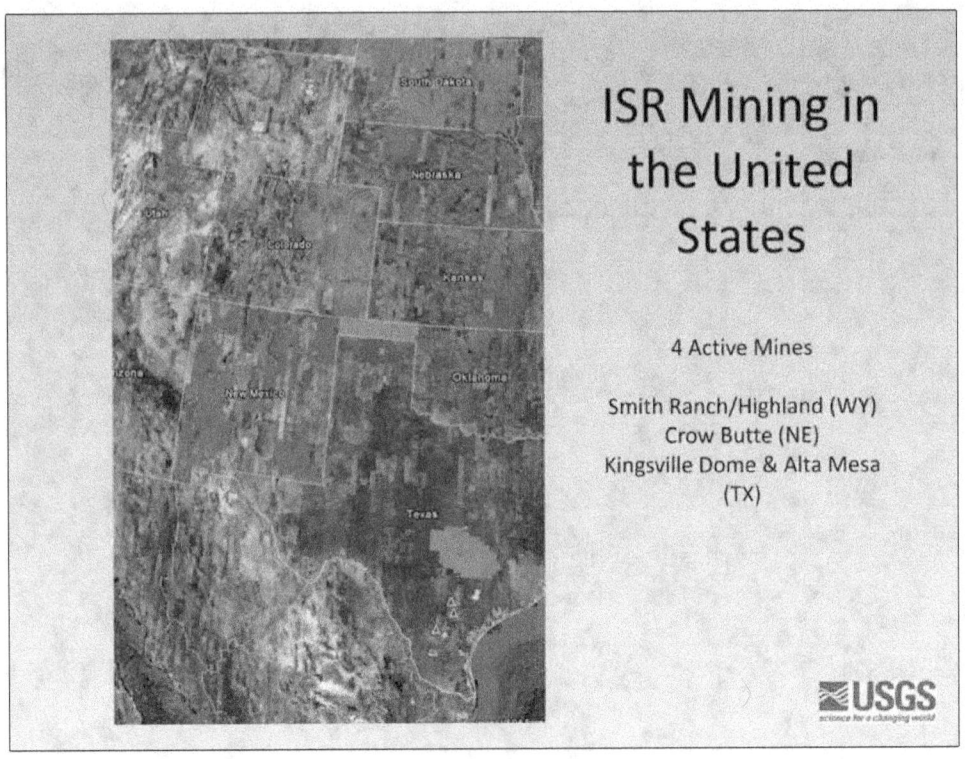

Background

The United States has been steadily producing uranium using ISR mining since the mid-1970s. In April 2009 there were four active mines in the United States (red markers): Cameco's Smith Ranch/Highland property in Wyoming and Crow Butte mine in Nebraska, and Mestena Uranium's Alta Mesa mine and URI's Kingsville Dome mine, both located in Texas.

Most uranium production from ISR mines has come from mines in Wyoming and Texas (green markers), with only pilot projects testing mining and restoration techniques developed in New Mexico (Crown Point, Mobil) and Colorado (Grover, Wyoming Minerals). More than 20 ISR mines anticipate or have begun the process of applying for licensing (yellow markers).

According to the Energy Information Agency, the United States imported 82 percent of its uranium in 2007 (Energy Information Agency, 2009) and 38 percent of U.S. uranium reserves are classified as ISR amenable (Nuclear Energy Agency, 2008). Thus, the safe and effective use of ISR technology in mining uranium deposits is a potentially critical element in the movement towards energy independence in the United States

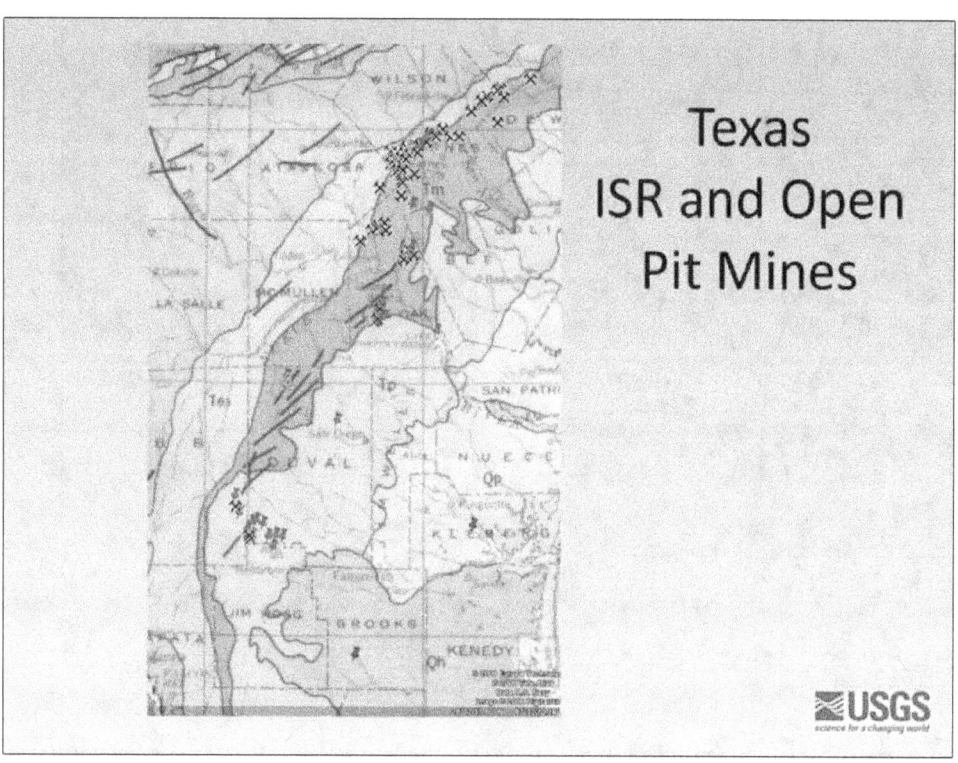

Texas Coastal Plain Uranium District

Historically, uranium in Texas has been produced from Tertiary units along the southwest coastal plain. Uranium was first mined from a series of open-pit deposits developed in the Whitsett Formation (Jackson Group) and Catahoula Formation, starting in the late 1950s, when uranium was discovered during radiometric surveys in support of oil and gas exploration in Texas.

Black crossed mine symbols are uranium properties identified by the USGS Mineral Resources Data System database (http://tin.er.usgs.gov/) and show mostly historical open-pit mines located near Karnes City, Texas. The green markers represent closed ISR mines, and the red markers indicate operating ISR mines as of April 2009.

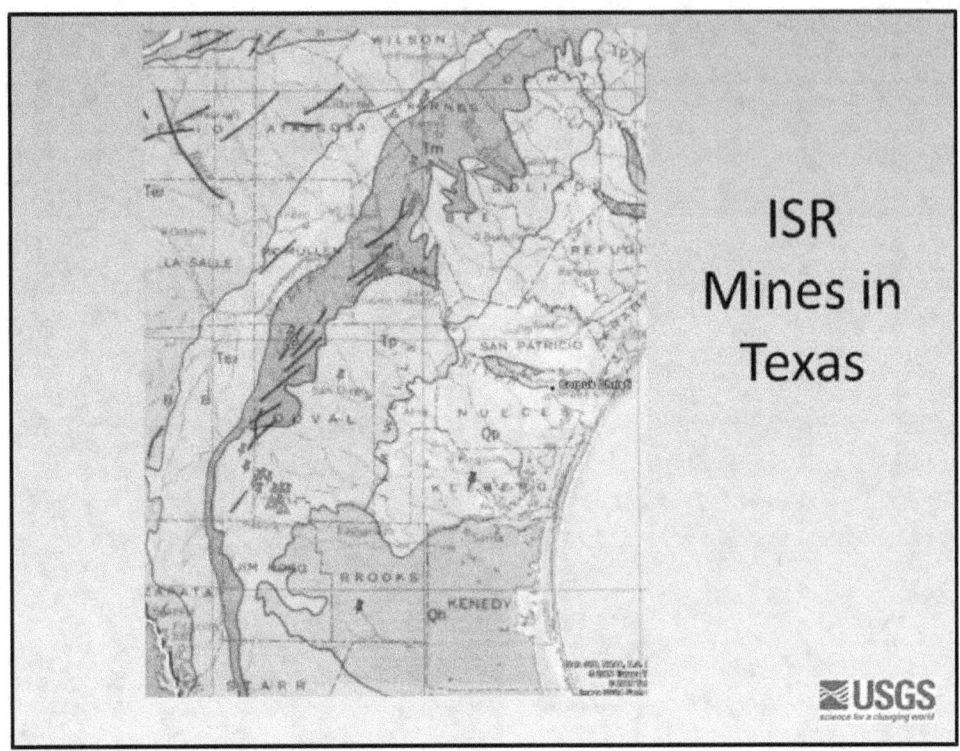

Along the southwest Texas coastal plain, uranium is mined, using ISR techniques, from the:
     —Goliad Formation (Tp); a series of Miocene mudstone, conglomerates, and limestones, which is host to seven ISR mines
     —Oakville Sandstone and Catahoula Formation (Tm); Miocene and Oligocene sandstone, clays, mudstones and Catahoula tuffs hosting 27 mines; 15 mines in the Oakville Sandstone and 13 mines in the Catahoula Formation
     —Whitsett Formation (Te, Jackson Group); Oligocene mudstones, sandstones and tuffs which host two mines.

Thirty-six sites were authorized in Texas; seven were never mined (orange triangles), one was a tailings project (white square), and one was combined with another property. This leaves 27 mines (green markers) that were developed by construction of 77 well fields, termed Production Authorization Areas (PAAs) in Texas. The term "well field" and "PAA" will be used interchangeably throughout this presentation. Baseline and "amended restoration" values are available for all 27 mines/ 77 PAAs in TCEQ records.

Currently two mines are active in Texas: the Kingsville Dome mine in Kleberg County, operated by Uranium Resources International (URI), and the Alta Mesa mine in Brooks County, operated by Mestena Uranium (red markers). Two mines are in standby or shut down (green markers): the Vasquez and Rosita mines, both URI properties in Duval County. Two ISR mines are in the process of being permitted (yellow markers): Goliad in Goliad County (Uranium Energy Corporation) and La Palangana, a South Texas Mining Ventures property in Duval County.

Table 1: Baseline Water Quality for Zamzow PAA-1

ATTACHMENT G

BASELINE WATER QUALITY TABLE

TEXAS WATER COMMISSION

GROUND WATER ANALYSIS REPORT SUMMARY
BASELINE WATER QUALITY – Solution Mining

Company: _IFC Corp_
Mine Name: _Zamzow_
Mine Area: _PAA-1 (New and Consolidated)_
Date Instantiated: _October 31, 1988_

BASELINE WATER QUALITY TABLE

	PARAMETER	UNIT	NON PRODUCTION ZONE Low	NON PRODUCTION ZONE Average	NON PRODUCTION ZONE High	MINE AREA Low	MINE AREA Average	MINE AREA High	PRODUCTION AREA Low	PRODUCTION AREA Average	PRODUCTION AREA High	WELL I.D. BY AREA NON PROD ZONE	WELL I.D. BY AREA Mine	WELL I.D. BY AREA Production
1	Calcium	mg/l				172	217	552	195	269	336			
2	Magnesium	mg/l				15	36.4	84.2	3.0	22.7	48		*	*
3	Sodium	mg/l				239	342	750	225	303	455			
4	Potassium	mg/l				13	36.5	49	14.3	26.7	50			
5	Carbonate	mg/l				0	0	0	0	0	0			
6	Bicarbonate	mg/l				128	267	400	157	249	346			
	Sulfate	mg/l				454	793	1,522	411	601	942			
	Chloride	mg/l				350	502	936	304	528	662			
9	Fluoride	mg/l				0.14	0.54	1.19	0.01	0.36	0.50			
10	Nitrate - N	mg/l				<0.01	0.16	0.9	<0.01	0.14	0.45			
11	Silica	mg/l				31	51.6	85	11	41.6	74			
12	pH	Std. unit				6.6	7.0	7.66	6.68	7.0	7.45			
13	TDS	mg/l				1,627	2,238	3,728	1,810	2,037	2,340			
14	Conductivity	umhos				2,720	3,204	4,300	2680	3,049	3,430			
15	Alkalinity	Std. unit				105	225	300	206	238	264			
16	Arsenic	mg/l				<0.001	0.009	0.01	<0.001	0.006	0.044			
17	Cadmium	mg/l				<0.0001	0.001	0.007	<0.0002	0.0035	0.0011			
18	Iron	mg/l				0.01	0.915	6.0	0.01	0.075	0.28			
19	Lead	mg/l				<0.001	0.001	0.906	<0.001	0.001	0.02			
20	Manganese	mg/l				0.007	0.224	0.82	0.01	0.11N	0.19			
21	Mercury	mg/l				<0.0002	0.0004	0.0018	0.0001	0.0004	0.001			
22	Selenium	mg/l				<0.001	0.01	0.01	<0.001	0.004	0.01			
23	Ammonia	mg/l				<0.001	0.271	1.4	<0.01	0.290	0.78			
24	Uranium	mg/l				<0.001	0.171	1.7	<0.001	0.079	0.435			
25	Molybdenum	mg/l				<0.001	0.03	0.66	<0.001	0.236	1.1			
26	Radium 226	pCi/l				1.5	335	959	9.5	352	744			

* LIST THE IDENTIFICATION NUMBERS OF WELLS USED TO OBTAIN THE LOW, AVERAGE AND HIGH VALUES   **MONITOR WELLS

USGS
science for a changing world

TCEQ ISR Restoration Database

The ISR restoration database is housed in the TCEQ offices in Austin, Texas. The database consists of binders for each mine in a data room adjacent to regulator offices. TCEQ does not represent these data as validated. Official data are on microfiche in an adjacent building, but the data are poorly organized and difficult to search. A digital database, compiled by a retired TCEQ employee, was also made available to the USGS. This digital database was cross-checked against original data sheets from the TCEQ data room, which forms the basis of this research.

TCEQ employees were extremely helpful in allowing the USGS full access to their data and copying facilities and were always available to answer questions about the database or permitting process.

This table is a typical data sheet summarizing pre-mining groundwater baseline data for a Texas PAA. In Texas, 26 chemical constituents are measured before mining to establish a baseline, as shown in Table 1. Restoration values are initially set as baseline, with operators selecting the highest average concentration from either the production or mine area as their restoration goal. At this Zamzow well field, PAA-1, 0.171 milligram per liter uranium was the highest average value from the mine or production area for uranium, as highlighted in Table 1.

Table 2 : Initial Restoration Table for Zamzow PAA-1

Table 2 is a copy of the initial restoration table for Zamzow PAA-1. Note that the restoration goal for uranium in groundwater is set as 0.171 milligram per liter, as highlighted on the table, which was the highest average uranium content from the PAA mine area, as shown on Table 1.

Table 3: Amended Restoration Table for Zamzow PAA-1

ATTACHMENT A

RESTORATION TABLE
(Amended)

Parameter	Unit	Concentration
Calcium	mg/l	317.
Magnesium	mg/l	38.4
Sodium	mg/l	450.
Potassium	mg/l	30.3
Carbonate	mg/l	0
Bicarbonate	mg/l	750.
Sulfate	mg/l	793.
Chloride	mg/l	538.
Fluoride	mg/l	0.54
Nitrate-N	mg/l	0.16
Silica	mg/l	51.6
pH	std. units	6.5 - 8.5
TDS	mg/l	2289.
Conductivity	μmhos	3204.
Alkalinity	std. units	500.
Arsenic	mg/l	0.2
Cadmium	mg/l	0.001
Iron	mg/l	0.915
Lead	mg/l	0.004
Manganese	mg/l	0.224
Mercury	mg/l	0.0006
Molybdenum	mg/l	5.
Selenium	mg/l	0.01
Uranium	mg/l	3.
Ammonia-N	mg/l	200.
Radium-226	pCi/l	200.

≋USGS
science for a changing world

All PAAs in Texas have received amended restoration goals for at least one element after operators have expended a reasonable degree of effort to restore groundwater, as determined by TCEQ regulators, following established guidelines. The final restoration table for Zamzow PAA-1 shows an amended limit of 3.00 milligrams per liter for uranium. This amended restoration value is believed to be a relatively arbitrary value set by the regulators, as illustrated by the number of PAAs that set amended values at rounded whole numbers that were unrelated to any restoration level actually achieved in the PAAs. As there are no "final sample" data for Zamzow PAA-1, no information is available to describe the degree to which this well field was restored.

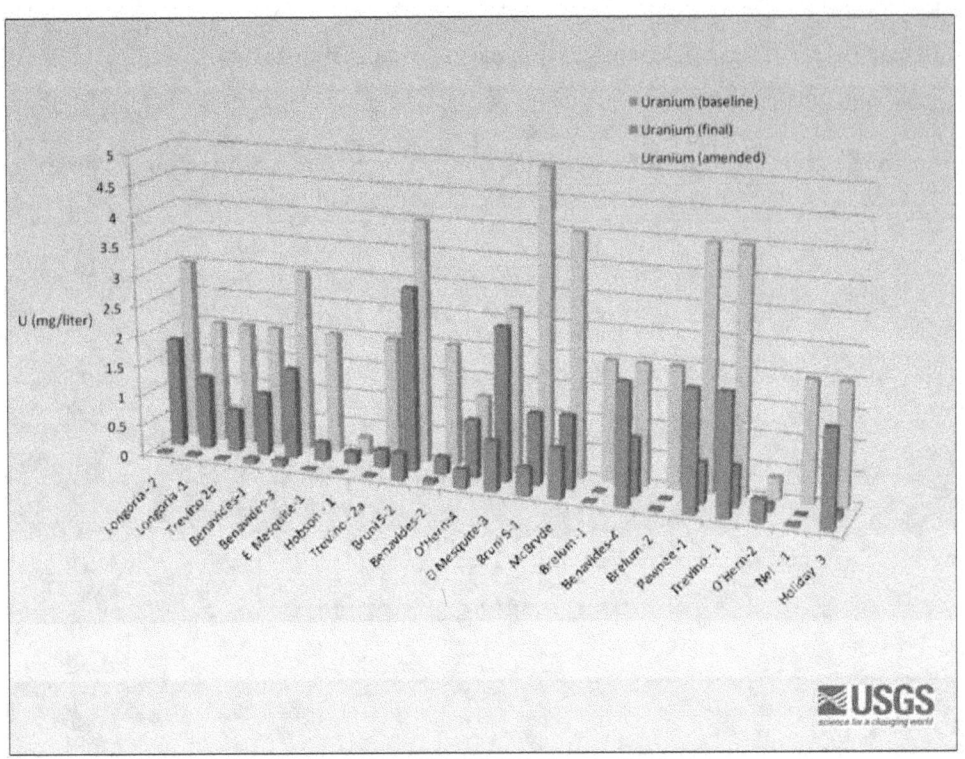

This graph of uranium concentration for various Texas PAAs illustrates the relationship between baseline, final values, and amended restoration goals in the PAAs where final values were available. The blue bars represent baseline restoration goals for uranium as set by the highest average uranium concentration in baseline samples from either the mine or the production area. Well-field designations are shown on the X-axis of this chart. Red bars represent "final values" for uranium prior to release of the PAAs, and green bars represent amended restoration goals for uranium. There is no clear relationship between the final value achieved for uranium in groundwater at the PAAs, and the amended restoration goals. Amended restoration goals do not reflect the degree of restoration achieved at the PAAs in Texas for which final values are available. Therefore, only those fields for which final values were available were chosen for this analysis.

Only 22 PAAs from 13 mines have final sample values. These 22 PAAs form the basis of the study of restoration at these well fields.

Table 4: Baseline Groundwater in United States ISR Mines – Constituents with EPA MCLs

Baseline Groundwater Characteristics of U.S. Uranium ISL Projects

Chemical Constituent (mg/L unless stated otherwise)	EPA MCL	Texas Baseline Range (71-77 PAAs)	Texas - Number of PAAs Where Average Baseline Exceeds MCL/total # of PAAs & percentage		New Mexico Crown Point ISL Pilot	Colorado Grover ISL Pilot	Wyoming (SR WFL, CR MU2-6, Irigaray MU1-5)	Nebraska Crow Butte (MU 1-5 & R&D Site)
USEPA Primary Maximum Contaminant Levels (MCLs):								
Arsenic	0.010	0.0010 - 0.2000	45/73	62 %	0.004	0.01	0.006	0.001
Barium	2	-	-	-	0.1	0.03	0.073	0.10
Cadmium	0.005	0.0001 - 0.126	21/73	29%	0.006	0.002	0.016	0.006
Chromium	0.1	-	-	-	0.007	0.003	0.259	0.01
Copper	1.3	-	-	-	0.01	0.06	0.043	0.012
Cyanide	0.2	-	-	-	0.088	-	-	-
Fluoride	4	0.2 - 2.0	0/73	0%	0.39	0.7	0.307	0.69
Gross Alpha (pCi/L)	15	-	-	-	-	87.67	-	-
Gross Beta (millirems/year)	4	-	-	-	-	15.23	-	-
Lead	0.015	0.001 - 1.970	35/73	48%	0.003	0.02	0.038	0.032
Mercury	0.002	0.00003 - 0.44500	6/73	8%	0.00024	0.0002	0.001	0.0007
Nitrate	10	0.01 - 12.0	1/77	1%	0.09	1.4	3.01	0.07
Nitrite	1	-	-	-	-	-	0.168	0.004
Radium ($^{226\ \&\ 228}$Ra: pCi/L)	5	5.45 - 1536.5	71/71	100%	<14.1	13.4	293.15	405.4
Selenium	0.05	0.001 - 0.600	7/73	10%	0.01	0.01	0.015	0.002
Uranium	0.03	0.002 - 2.913	66/73	90%	0.01	0.086	0.193	0.103

Baseline Characterization of Groundwater in U.S. ISR Well Fields

Baseline standards for all 77 Texas PAAs can be used to characterize Texas ISR well fields that serve as a basis of comparison with baseline values determined for other ISR well fields in the United States. The argument is commonly made that before mining, groundwater in ISR well fields is so contaminated that it should not be used for human consumption. Before mining, these aquifers are typically granted exemptions from the Clean Water Act, termed aquifer exemptions, by the U.S. Environmental Protection Agency (USEPA).

In Texas, more than 25 percent of PAAs are characterized by baseline groundwater above the maximum contaminant level (MCL) for arsenic, cadmium, lead, radium, and uranium (shown highlighted on Table 4). MCL is set by the U.S. Environmental Protection Agency (USEPA; http://www.epa.gov/safewater/contaminants/index.html) for those elements with well-established links to negative human health effects. All PAAs contain radium above MCL, and 90 percent contain uranium above MCL. Although baseline is artificially elevated in this database because the operator is selecting the highest average value within the production or mine area, this value does serve to identify elements of concern in these well fields.

In the Crown Point pilot project in New Mexico, only cadmium was elevated above MCL. At the Grover pilot project in Colorado, baseline water showed gross alpha, gross beta, radium, and uranium above MCL. In Wyoming, averaged values for the Smith Ranch 1, Christensen Ranch 2-6, and Irigaray 1-5 mine units were elevated above MCL for cadmium, chromium, lead, radium, and uranium.
In Nebraska (Crow Butte mine units 1-5 and the Crow Butte R &D site), average cadmium, lead, radium, and uranium were elevated above MCL. Elements above MCL are highlighted in the table.

With the exception of the New Mexico deposit (Crown Point), these well fields are characterized by groundwater elevated in multiple MCLs prior to mining. Radium is almost always elevated above MCL while uranium is typically elevated and cadmium and lead commonly elevated. These well fields would require pretreatment to be used as a source for drinking water.

Table 5: Baseline Groundwater in U.S. ISR Mines – Constituents with EPA Secondary (recommended) Standards

Baseline Groundwater Characteristics of U.S. Uranium ISL Projects

Chemical Constituent (mg/L unless stated otherwise)	EPA Secondary Standard	Texas Baseline Range (71-77 PAAs)	Texas - Number of PAAs Where Average Baseline Exceeds Secondary Standards/total # of PAAs & Percentage (highlighted if > 25% of PAAs Exceed Secondary Standards)		New Mexico Crown Point ISL Pilot	Colorado Grover ISL Pilot	Wyoming ISR WF1, CR MU3-6, Irigaray MU2-5)	Nebraska Crow Butte (MU 1-9 & R&D Site)
EPA Secondary Recommended Standards:								
Aluminum	0.200	-	-	-	0.02	0.537	0.117	-
Chloride	250	122.5 - 3505.0	64/77	83 %	20.3	7	9.8	202.6
Iron	0.30	0.01 - 6.3	32/72	44 %	0.67	0.7	0.648	0.04
Manganese	0.05	0.01 - 5.06	37/73	51%	0.05	0.02	0.018	0.03
Silver	0.10	-	-	-	<0.01	0.003	-	-
Sulfate	250	10.3 - 1197	10/77	13 %	38	38.3	300	353
Total Dissolved Solids	500	628 - 6349	73/73	100 %	357	295	616	1177
Zinc	5	-	-	-	0.01	0.04	0.073	0.017

Recommended secondary standards are set by the USEPA for constituents that, in high enough concentrations, negatively affect the esthetic quality of groundwater, but are not conclusively linked to any negative human health effect. Of those elements for which secondary standards are set by the USEPA, iron, sulfate, and total dissolved solids (TDS) are commonly elevated above recommended levels in pre-mining water at ISR facilities. Chloride and manganese are commonly high in Texas PAAs before mining, while TDS is elevated above the recommended standard in all pre-mining Texas PAAs. Elements elevated above secondary standards are highlighted in Table 5.

Table 6: Baseline Groundwater in U.S. ISR Mines – Constituents with no MCL or Secondary Standard

Baseline Groundwater Characteristics of U.S. Uranium ISR Projects

Chemical Constituent (mg/L unless stated otherwise)	USEPA MCL	Texas Baseline Range (71-77 PAAs)	New Mexico Crown Point ISR Pilot	Colorado Grover ISR Pilot	Wyoming (ISR WF1, CR-MU2-6, Irigaray MU1-5)	Nebraska Crow Butte (MU 1-5 & R&D Site)
No Established MCL or Recommended Secondary Standard:						
Alkalinity (as CaCO₃)	-	24 - 349	-	154.7	116.1	-
Ammonia-N	-	0.01 - 7.49	0.47	0.25	0.344	0.26
Bicarbonate	-	125 - 500	228	220.1	171.6	344
Boron	-	-	0.1	0.1	0.1	0.93
Calcium	-	0.2 - 395	5.8	9.1	29.4	12.97
Carbonate	-	0.10 - 38	-	4.31	22.4	369
Cobalt	-	-	<0.05	-		
Conductivity (umhos/cm)	-	1,110 - 11,160	-	380.7	1051	1947
Magnesium	-	0.48 - 150.0	-	1.1	5.324	3.27
Molybdenum	-	0.01 - 2.53	0.172	0.02	0.100	0.05
Nickel	-	-	0.02	0.2	0.093	0.03
Phosphorous	-	-	-	0.05		-
Potassium	-	6.38 - 101.1	-	4.43	9.810	13.10
Silica	-	15 - 98	-	5.45	10.496	16.7
Sodium	-	174 - 2,356	114	85.2	155	410
Thorium	-	-	-	0.7417		-

Table 6 shows average concentrations and a range of concentrations in Texas PAAs, within pre-mining baseline groundwater for those analytes for which no primary or secondary standards have been set by the USEPA.

Analyte	USEPA and TCEQ Drinking Water Standards (mg/l)	Baseline Range	Post-Restoration Range	PAAs with Baseline Above MCL or Recommended Standards	PAAs with Post-Restoration Water Above MCL or Recommended Standards	PAAs Where Post-Restoration Analyses Exceed Baseline	PAAs Where Post-Restoration Analyses are Below Baseline
Table 7: Groundwater Chemistry of Texas In-situ Uranium Production Authorization Areas							
(22 PAAs where final analyses are available)							
USEPA and TCEQ Primary Maximum Contaminant Levels (MCLs):							
Arsenic	0.01	.004 - 0.23	.002 - .323	77%	55%	18%	82%
Cadmium	0.005	0.0001 - 0.0126	0.0001 - 0.01	45%	23%	27%	73%
Fluoride	4	0.21 - 1.8	0.29 - 1.6	0%	0%	31%	69%
Lead	0.02	0.003 - 1.97	0.001 - 0.05	81%	18%	9%	91%
Mercury	0.002	0.0001 - 0.445	0.0001 - 0.01	9%	0%	22%	64%
Nitrate	10	0.031 - 10.0	0.001 - 2.8	0%	0%	4%	96%
Selenium	0.05	0.001 - 0.049	0.001 - 0.102	18%	4%	54%	45%
Radium (226 & 228 Ra: Pci/l)	5 pci/l	9.36 - 429.8	5.2 - 149	100%	100%	4%	96%
Uranium	0.03	0.025 - 2.0	0.013 - 3.02	95%	86%	68%	32%
TCEQ Secondary Recommended Standards							
Sulfate	300	15.8 - 250	78 - 3881	0%	18%	86%	14%
Chloride	300	196.9 - 3505	138 - 3326	86%	86%	22%	78%
Total Dissolved Solids	1000	785.7 - 6349	706.3 - 6155	81%	77%	31%	55%
Iron	0.3	0.04 - 5.49	0.01 - 2.7	54%	9%	4%	96%
Manganese	0.05	0.01 - 0.41	0.01 - 0.84	77%	50%	40%	60%
No Established MCL or Secondary Standards							
Calcium	-	4.13 - 241	14.7 - 191			77%	23%
Magnesium	-	0.477 - 125	2.27 - 53			72%	28%
Sodium	-	200 - 2356	169 - 2247			31%	65%
Potassium	-	6.38 - 101	6.1 - 70			14%	86%
Carbonate	-	0.1 - 17.9	0 - 14.6			50%	30%
Bicarbonate	-	160 - 500	160 - 500			66%	25%
Silica	-	16.3 - 76	13.4 - 77.6			19%	81%
Conductivity (umhos/cm)	-	1310 - 11160	1429 - 3697			76%	24%
Alkalinity (as CaCO3)	-	134 - 349	145 - 408			81%	10%
Molybdenum	-	0.01 - 0.2	0.0001 - 3.38			42%	54%
Ammonia-N	-	0.01 - 7.49	0.04 - 120			76%	24%

Baseline and post-restoration data was available for all 22 PAAs with the exception of Ra, Mo, K, Si, Bicarbonate, Ammonia (21); Conductivity (14); Alkalinity (11) & Carbonate (10)

Restoration Results for Texas PAAs

Table 7 shows the average value, post-restoration, and baseline ranges of chemical constituents for all 22 well fields that have post-restoration analyses in the TCEQ records.

In general, at PAAs where post-restoration values exceed MCL, the elements elevated in baseline values (As, Cd, Pb, Se, Ra, and U) continue to be elevated after mining.

As compared to baseline values for the PAAs, uranium and selenium are elevated in the majority of PAAs. More than half of PAAs show a decrease in As, Cd, Fl, Pb, Hg, nitrate, and Ra after mining.

The following slides examine these trends in detail.

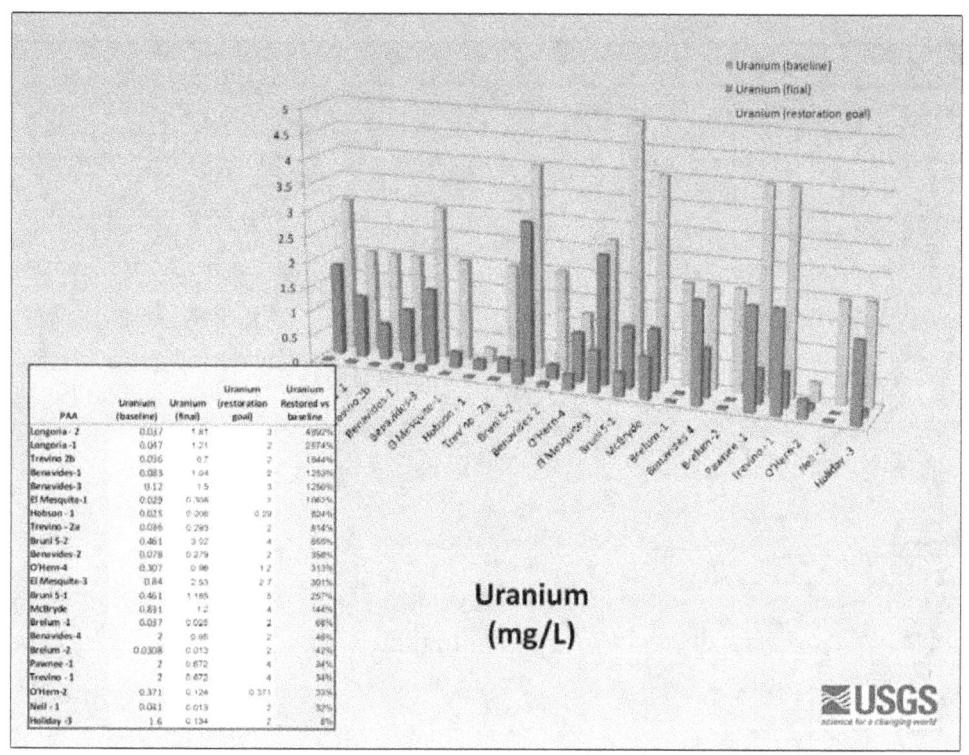

The USEPA-established MCL for uranium in drinking water is 0.03 milligram per liter. Ninety-five percent of Texas PAAs have a baseline value above MCL. Only the Hobson-1 and El Mesquite–1 PAAs were below the MCL for uranium and El Mesquite "rounded out" to equal MCL.

Eighty-six percent of Texas PAAs show a final restoration above MCL. In 68 percent of PAAs, final value exceeded baseline, and in 32 percent of PAAs, restoration was below baseline for uranium.

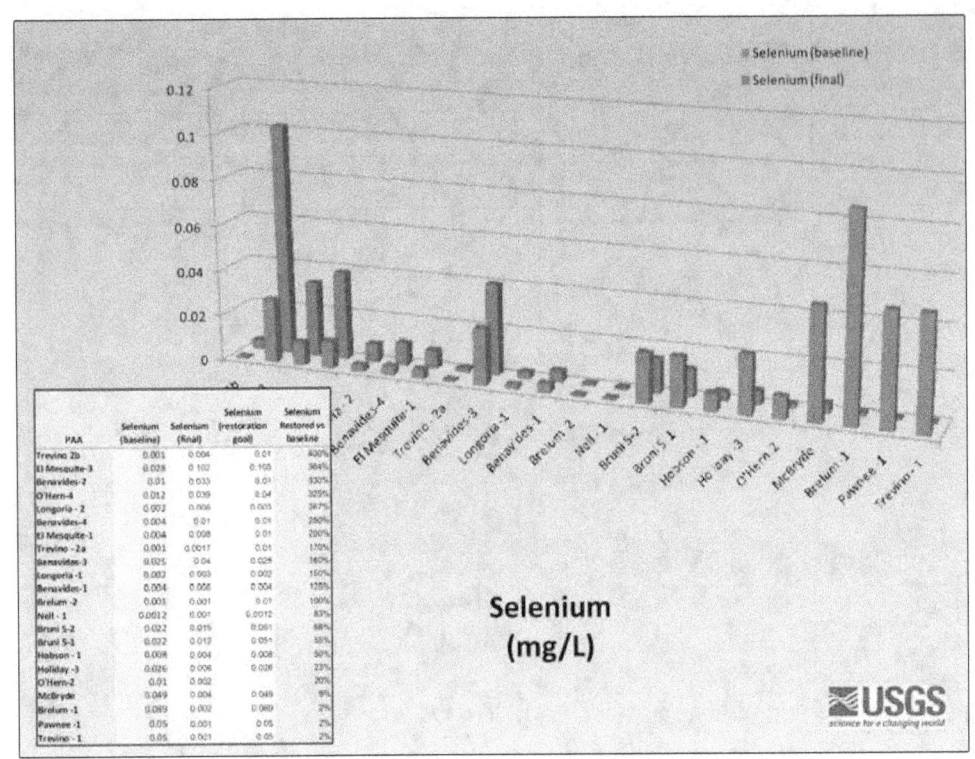

The MCL for selenium is 0.05 milligram per liter in drinking water. In 18 percent of PAAs, baseline of groundwater was above MCL, and in 24 percent of PAAs, the final restoration value was above MCL. After mining and restoration, 55 percent of PAAs exceeded baseline and 45 percent of PAAs were below baseline.

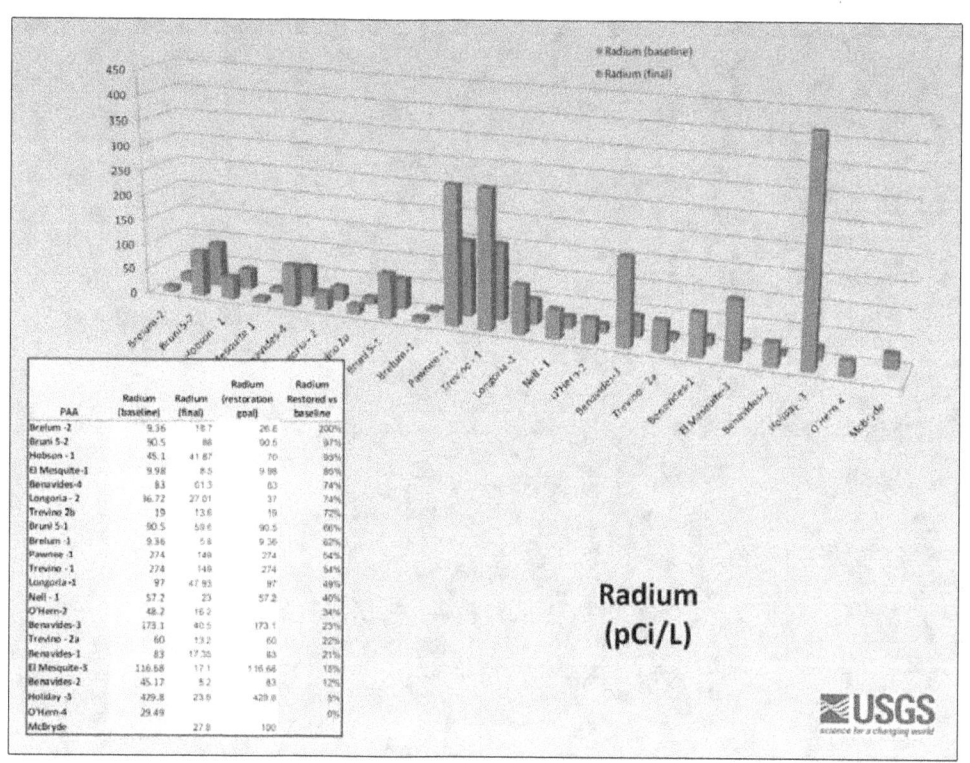

The MCL for radium (^{226}Ra and ^{228}Ra) is 5 pCi/L in drinking water. All PAAs are characterized by baseline and post-restoration radium concentrations above MCL.

After mining and restoration, 4 percent of PAAs were above baseline, and 96 percent of PAAs were below baseline.

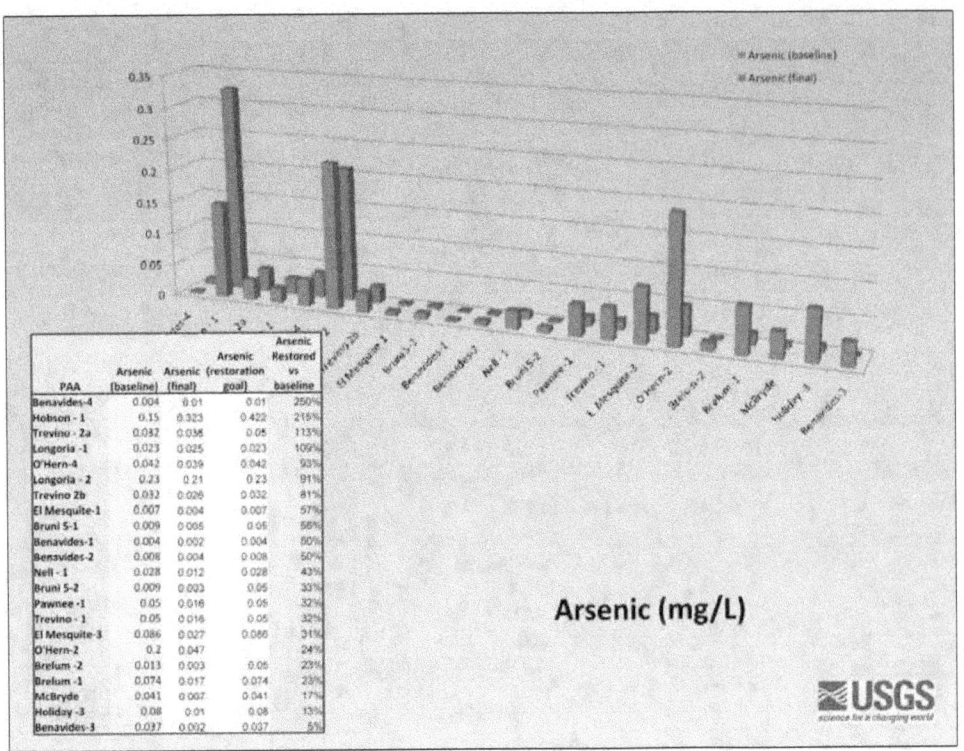

PAA	Arsenic (baseline)	Arsenic (final)	Arsenic (restoration goal)	Arsenic Restored vs baseline
Benavides-4	0.004	0.01	0.01	250%
Hobson - 1	0.15	0.323	0.422	215%
Trevino - 2a	0.032	0.036	0.05	113%
Longoria -1	0.023	0.025	0.023	109%
O'Hern-4	0.042	0.039	0.042	93%
Longoria - 2	0.23	0.21	0.23	91%
Trevino 2b	0.032	0.026	0.032	81%
El Mesquite-1	0.007	0.004	0.007	57%
Bruni 5-1	0.009	0.005	0.05	56%
Benavides-1	0.004	0.002	0.004	50%
Benavides-2	0.008	0.004	0.008	50%
Nell - 1	0.028	0.012	0.028	43%
Bruni 5-2	0.009	0.003	0.05	33%
Pawnee -1	0.05	0.016	0.05	32%
Trevino - 1	0.05	0.016	0.05	32%
El Mesquite-3	0.086	0.027	0.086	31%
O'Hern-2	0.2	0.047		24%
Brelum -2	0.013	0.003	0.05	23%
Brelum -1	0.074	0.017	0.074	23%
McBryde	0.041	0.007	0.041	17%
Holiday -3	0.08	0.01	0.08	13%
Benavides-3	0.037	0.002	0.037	5%

Arsenic (mg/L)

The MCL for arsenic is 0.01 milligram per liter in drinking water. Before mining, 77 percent of PAAs showed arsenic above the MCL, and after restoration 55 percent of PAAs were above the MCL.

After restoration, 18 percent of PAAs exceeded baseline and 82 percent of PAAs were below baseline.

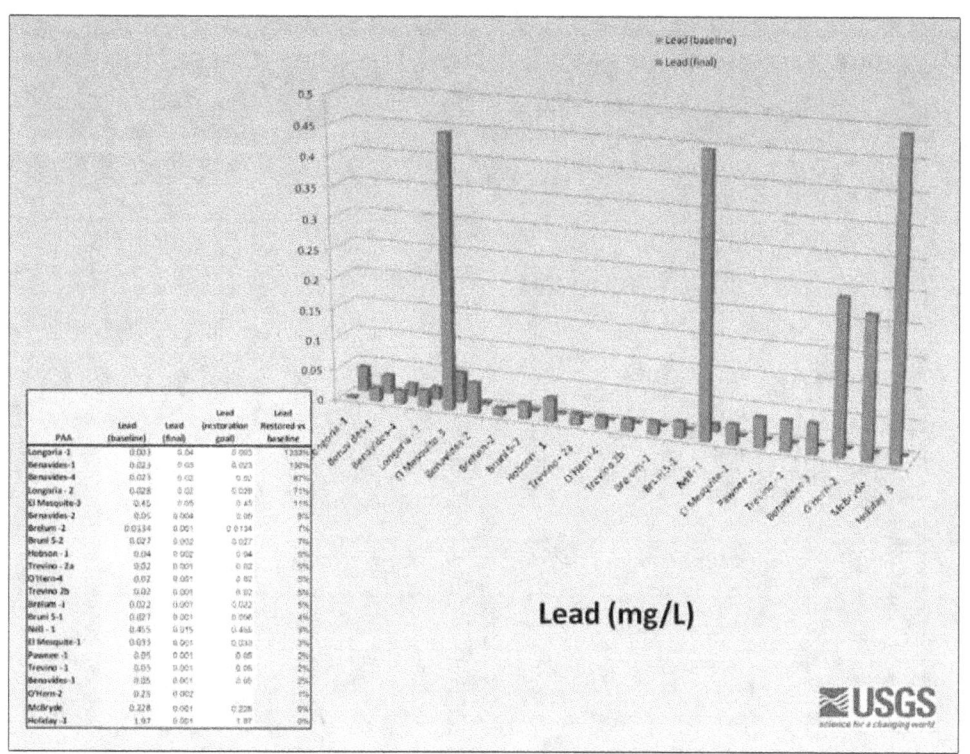

The MCL for lead is 0.02 milligram per liter in drinking water. Eighty-one percent of PAAs have baseline levels above MCL, and 18 percent of PAAs are characterized by final restoration values above MCL.

After mining and reclamation, 9 percent of PAAs were above baseline and 91 percent of PAAs were below baseline.

Although restoration results vary widely for individual well fields, among the elements with an MCL, only selenium and uranium show overall increases in post-restoration groundwater in more than 50 percent of PAAs (Table 7). Of constituents for which secondary standards are established by the USEPA, sulfate increased in the majority of well fields after mining and restoration, whereas chloride, TDS, iron, and manganese decreased in the majority of well fields.

Of those chemical constituents for which there are no established MCLs or secondary standards, calcium, magnesium, bicarbonate, conductivity, carbonate, alkalinity and ammonia increased; sodium, potassium and silica decreased in the majority of well fields after mining and restoration. Statistically, molybdenum decreased in the small majority of well fields after mining.

Has Groundwater Been Restored to Baseline at Uranium In-situ Recovery Mines S. Texas Coastal Plain ?

- No PAA Returned All Analytes to Baseline

- In 2 PAAs all MCL Elements Returned to Baseline or Lower:
    - O'Hern-2
    - Trevino-1

- In 1 PAA All Analytes With Established MCL or Recommended Secondary Standards Returned to Baseline:
    - O'Hern-2

USGS
science for a changing world

Regarding the original question of whether or not groundwater has been restored to baseline in Texas uranium ISR well fields, it was observed that no well field for which final sample results were found in TCEQ records returned every element to baseline. However, two PAAs returned all elements for which USEPA has established MCLs to baseline: the O'Hern-2 and Trevino-1 PAAs.

Trevino-1, which was mined from the Oakville Sandstone and restored using electrodialysis, shows restored sulfate to 164 percent of baseline. Reclamation at O'Hern-2 returned constituents with secondary standards or MCLs to baseline values or below.

Table 8: Baseline and Final Chemistry of Groundwater at the O'Hern PAA-2 Well Field

O'Hern-2 Groundwater Sweep and Reverse Osmosis	Analyte	Baseline	Final
Analytes for which EPA and TCEQ have set Maximum Contaminant Levels	Arsenic	0.2	0.047
	Cadmium	0.01	0.0005
	Fluoride	1.37	0.73
	Lead	0.25	0.002
	Mercury	0.445	0.0001
	Nitrate-N	0.86	0.47
	Selenium	0.01	0.002
	Radium	48.2	16.2
	Uranium	0.371	0.124
Analytes for which TCEQ has set Secondary Recommended Upper Limits	Sulfate	129	102
	Chloride	254	220
	TDS	979	890
	Iron	3.52	0.02
	Manganese	0.124	0.03
	Ca	13.7	14.7
	Mg	2.7	2.27
	Na	310	289
	K	9.7	6.6
	Carbonate	1.78	2.6
	Bicarbonate	347	
	Silica	43.7	35
	Conductivity	1626	1429
	Alkalinity		
	Ammonia-N	0.77	0.3
	Molybdenum	1.1	0.24

Specifically looking at restoration details from the O'Hern PAA-2 , this well field was developed by Cogema from 1979 to1982 in the Catahoula Formation. Groundwater sweep and reverse osmosis were both used to restore groundwater after mining. Calcium and carbonate were both slightly elevated above baseline following mining and reclamation, as shown in Table 8 above.

The aquifer overlying O'Hern-2 is characterized by an average calcium of 27 milligrams per liter and carbonate of 10.1 milligrams per liter, so post-restoration elevation of these elements in the O'Hern-2 PAA seems inconsequential in the scheme of local hydrochemistry. No final values for bicarbonate or alkalinity were reported, so the specific degree to which this PAA was restored is unknown.

There is a notation in the TCEQ database that O'Hern PAA-3 did not receive any amendments. However, this could not be corroborated by TCEQ records.

Long-Term Stability and Natural Attenuation

In Texas, after ISR mining ceased and restoration of the well fields was completed, PAAs were monitored for a minimum of 6 months. This period of monitoring has recently been increased to one year if no amendments to the restoration table are requested, and to two years if the operator requests an amendment to the restoration table.

Some well fields monitored for longer periods of time during the post-mining and remediation stability period show trends of increasing analyte concentration, as noted by USGS geologists while examining records at pilot projects in Colorado (Grover), New Mexico (Crown Point), and throughout Wyoming.

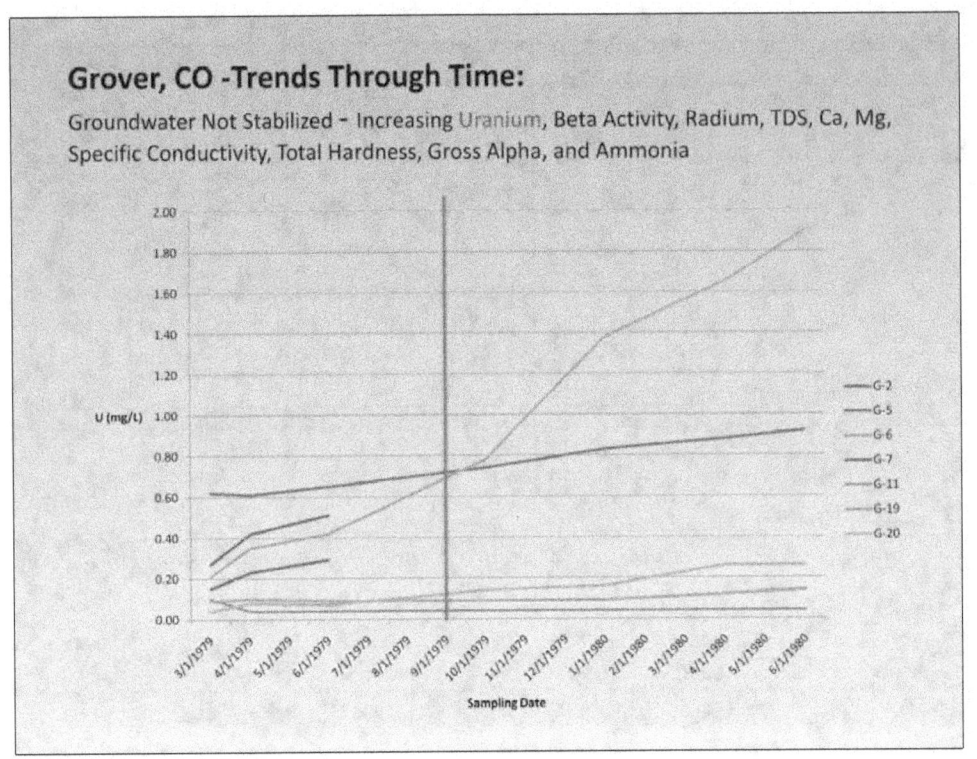

Grover, CO -Trends Through Time:

Groundwater Not Stabilized − Increasing Uranium, Beta Activity, Radium, TDS, Ca, Mg, Specific Conductivity, Total Hardness, Gross Alpha, and Ammonia

At the Grover, Colorado, pilot test site, pump and treat technologies did not return groundwater to baseline. Analysis of data collected by Colorado State regulators showed upward-trending uranium, beta activity, radium, TDS, calcium, magnesium, specific conductivity, total hardness, gross alpha, and ammonia. Results from individual wells differentiated using solid colored lines are shown above in the time series plot of uranium concentration. Note that the vertical red line indicates the end of the 6-month stabilization period required for Texas PAAs. These increasing concentrations of analytes indicate groundwater may not have stabilized when the Grover well field was released.

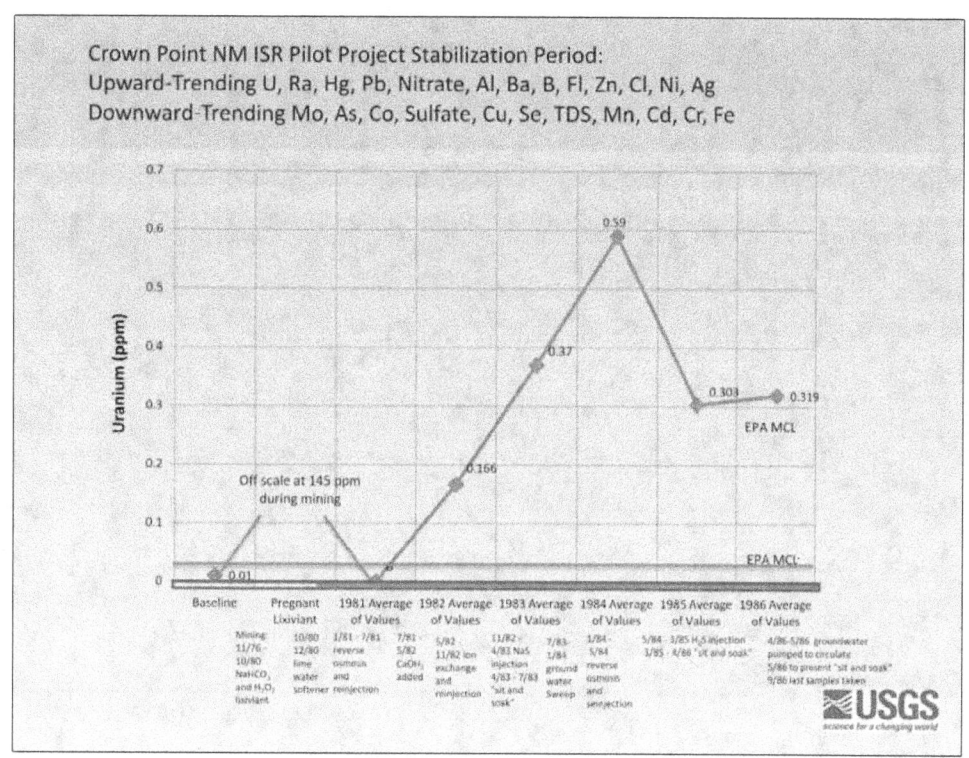

During the one-year stabilization period that followed restoration at Mobil's Crown Point, New Mexico ISR pilot project, both upward and downward trends in various chemical constituents were noted (Mobil, 1981). The Crown Point data are not detailed enough to analyze these trends, but the data indicate that groundwater may not have stabilized when the final samples were collected, similar to the Grover, Colorado, project.

Examples from Grover, Colorado, Crown Point, New Mexico, and ISR pilot projects in Wyoming indicate that the 6-month stability period mandated by Texas ISR rules may not have been long enough to adequately determine if groundwater in well fields had stabilized. Recent rule changes in Texas allow for longer term monitoring and could yield valuable data about the chemical stability of groundwater after ISR mining.

Remediation
of ISR Well Fields

- Groundwater Sweep
- Reverse Osmosis and Ion Exchange and Reinjection
- Reducing Agents (NaS, H_2S)
- Bioremediation

Effectiveness of Restoration Techniques

After mining has ceased, a restoration method called groundwater sweep can be used whereby groundwater in a mined aquifer is pumped from the well field either to a deeper aquifer, an adjacent well field where mining is being initiated, or to surface ponds where it is allowed to evaporate. Local groundwater then "sweeps in" to replace the displaced water. This is typically the first method of restoration applied to a well field (Mays, 1994).

Reverse osmosis and ion exchange are methods of removing contaminants from groundwater in well fields. The cleaned water is then reinjected into the well fields (Mays, 1994).

Reducing agents (H, NaS and H_2S) have been added to well-field groundwater in an attempt to return groundwater and host rocks to reducing conditions, thereby reversing the effects of oxidizing mining solutions (lixiviants) within the aquifer.

Bioremediation, the stimulation of native bacteria within the aquifer whose life processes fix metals from solution, is another remediation technique currently receiving much attention (Long and others, 2008).

PAA	Restoration Method	Arsenic	Cadmium	Fluoride	Lead	Mercury	Nitrate-N	Selenium	Radium	Uranium
Hobson - 1	GW Sweep Only	215%	1%	134%	5%	16%	9%	50%	93%	824%
Longoria -1	GW Sweep Only	109%	10000%	98%	1333%	333%	34%	150%	49%	2574%
Longoria - 2	GW Sweep Only	91%	10000%	82%	71%	333%	22%	267%	74%	4892%
McBryde	GW Sweep Only	17%	6%	50%	0%	10%	56%	8%		144%
Average for GW Sweep Only		**108%**	**5002%**	**91%**	**353%**	**173%**	**30%**	**119%**	**72%**	**2109%**
Benavides-4	RO	250%	3333%	77%	87%	100%	3%	250%	74%	48%
Bruni 5-1	RO	56%	2%	143%	4%	11%	15%	55%	66%	257%
Bruni 5-2	RO	33%	4%	155%	7%	11%	22%	68%	97%	655%
O'Hern-4	RO	93%	91%	63%	5%	13%	NR	325%	NR	313%
Average for RO only		**108%**	**858%**	**110%**	**26%**	**34%**	**13%**	**175%**	**79%**	**318%**
El Mesquite-1	RO and Ion Exchange	57%	17%	117%	3%	50%	22%	200%	85%	1062%
El Mesquite-3	RO and Ion Exchange	31%	83%	74%	11%	40%	19%	364%	15%	301%
Holiday -3	RO and Ion Exchange	13%	200%	94%	0%	100%	53%	23%	5%	8%
Average for RO and ion exchange		**34%**	**100%**	**95%**	**5%**	**63%**	**31%**	**196%**	**35%**	**457%**
Brelum -1	GW Sweep and RO	23%	6%	107%	5%	10%	3%	2%	82%	68%
Brelum -2	GW Sweep and RO	23%	1%	97%	7%	11%	5%	100%	200%	42%
O'Hern-2	GW Sweep and RO	24%	5%	53%	1%	0%	55%	20%	34%	33%
Average for GW Sweep and RO		**23%**	**4%**	**86%**	**4%**	**7%**	**21%**	**41%**	**99%**	**48%**
Trevino - 1	Electrodialysis	32%	1%	82%	2%	5%	5%	2%	54%	34%
Trevino - 2a	Electrodialysis	113%	1%	83%	5%	33%	6%	170%	22%	814%
Trevino 2b	Electrodialysis	81%	1%	81%	5%	33%	19%	400%	72%	1944%
Average for Electrodialysis		**75%**	**1%**	**82%**	**4%**	**24%**	**10%**	**191%**	**49%**	**931%**

Table 9: Elements with USEPA and TECQ Primary Maximum Contaminant Levels Restored vs. Baseline for Texas Well Fields With Known Restoration Methods

Pump and Treat Technology

Texas provides a database that can be used to examine the effectiveness of the "pump and treat" technologies of groundwater sweep, reverse osmosis, ion exchange, and electrodialysis. Historically, pump and treat techniques were the only restoration techniques used in ISR mines developed in Texas.

Uranium in groundwater is 2,109 percent of baseline in well fields using groundwater sweep only, yet is 48 percent of baseline when groundwater sweep is combined with reverse osmosis (Table 9). Similar trends are shown for arsenic, cadmium, lead, mercury, and selenium. Trends for fluoride and nitrate are not as clear.

Analysis of patterns in Texas PAAs show restoration using groundwater sweep coupled with reverse osmosis results in the greatest decrease in concentration of chemical constituents. These coupled techniques are commonly used in many well-field restoration projects nationwide.

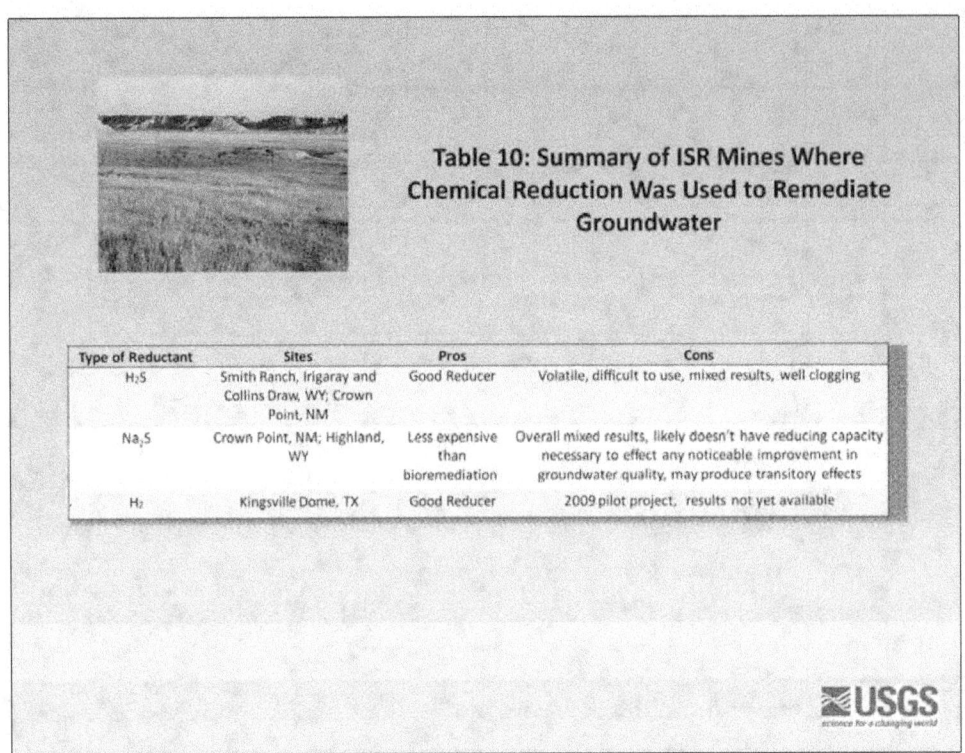

Table 10: Summary of ISR Mines Where Chemical Reduction Was Used to Remediate Groundwater

Type of Reductant	Sites	Pros	Cons
H_2S	Smith Ranch, Irigaray and Collins Draw, WY; Crown Point, NM	Good Reducer	Volatile, difficult to use, mixed results, well clogging
Na_2S	Crown Point, NM; Highland, WY	Less expensive than bioremediation	Overall mixed results, likely doesn't have reducing capacity necessary to effect any noticeable improvement in groundwater quality, may produce transitory effects
H_2	Kingsville Dome, TX	Good Reducer	2009 pilot project, results not yet available

Chemical Reduction

Inorganic chemical reductants are designed to reverse the effects of oxidizing lixiviant solutions on host rock and groundwater. Overall, these techniques when used in remediation of U.S. ISR mines, show mixed results (Table 10). Crown Point and Irigaray did not appear to significantly benefit from the addition of reductants into groundwater at the levels applied (LQD/DEQ Response Document, 2005; Mobil, 1981). Uranium Resources International is completing a pilot project in Texas to test the restoration effectiveness of hydrogen gas in removing analytes from groundwater (M. Pelliza, oral commun., May 2009). Results of this study are not yet available.

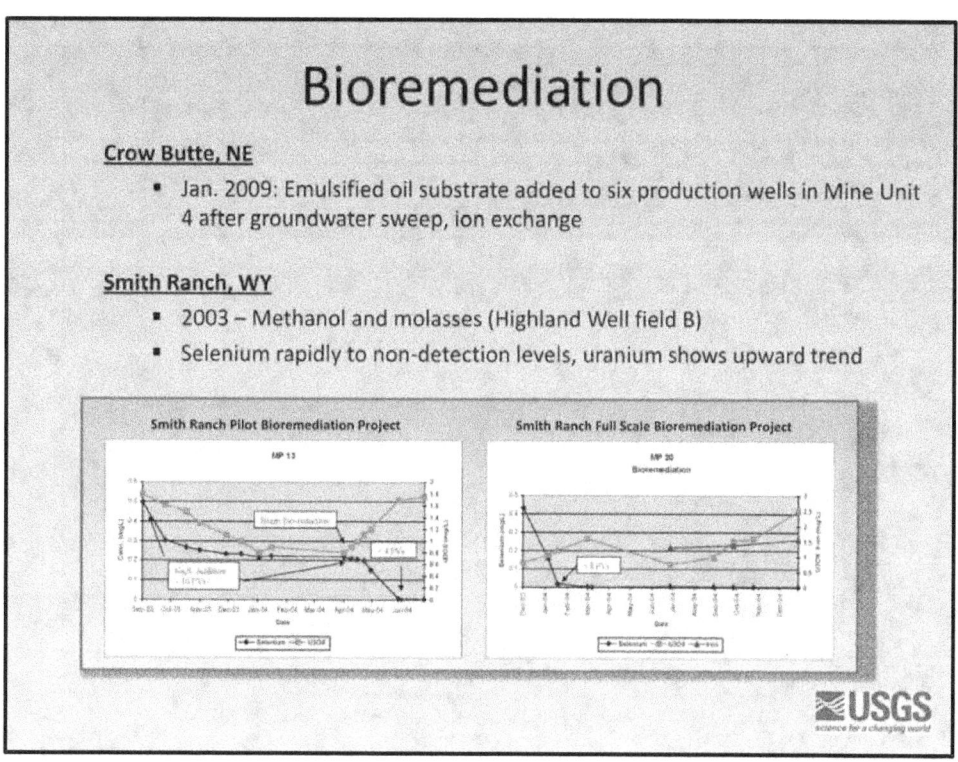

Bioremediation

Nutrients, such as acetate, methanol, and molasses, can be added to groundwater as a food source to stimulate native bacteria populations. As bacteria populations rise in response to increased food, metal concentrations decrease in groundwater; however the exact mechanism is uncertain.

In January 2009, an emulsified oil substrate was added to 6 production wells at the Crow Butte ISR mine as part of remediation of groundwater in Mine Unit 4 (NDEQ, 2009). The first 4 months of preliminary results do not show a significant reduction in uranium. At a Smith Ranch/Highland ISR remediation project in 2003, methanol and molasses were added to wells in the Highland B well field, first as a pilot project following chemical reduction (Na_2S) and then in a full-scale remediation project without prior chemical reduction (Reimann and Huffman, 2005). Selenium in groundwater was rapidly reduced in both the pilot (MP13) and full-scale (MP20) fields, although uranium concentration initially increased (see graphs above). Uranium increases noted in groundwater after bioremediation had been initiated may be attributable to the dissolution of iron oxyhydroxides and the concomitant release of their contained uranium in response to increasingly reducing conditions created during bioremediation (Reimann and Huffman, 2005). In subsequent bioremediation projects at Smith Ranch, cheese whey coupled with methanol has been used as a biostimulant.

The USGS continues to gather and process records from State agencies to track the effectiveness of these bioremediation methods.

Has any ISR Mine in the United States Returned Post-mining Groundwater to Baseline?

	More than half of PAAs were lower than baseline after mining and reclamation	More than half of PAAs were higher than baseline after mining and reclamation
MCLs	As, Cd, Fl, Pb, Hg, Nitrate, Ra	U, Se
Secondary Standards	Cl, TDS, Fe, Mn	Sulfate
Other Chemical Constituents	Na, K, Si, Mo	Ca, Mg, Bicarbonate, Conductivity, Alkalinity, Ammonia-N

Conclusions

Can we answer the question: "Has any ISR mine in the United States returned post-mining groundwater to baseline?"
Answer: Not based upon analysis of the Texas database because "final value" records were found for only 22 of 77 PAAs (13 of 36 mines).

We can conclude that in Texas, ISR mines are characterized by high baseline arsenic, cadmium, lead, selenium, radium, and uranium. After mining and restoration, for those well fields that reported "final values" in TCEQ records, more than half of the PAAs had lowered levels of many elements, including some that dropped below MCL.

Of those elements for which MCL is established, the majority of PAAs showed increases in uranium and selenium after mining and restoration and decreases in arsenic, cadmium, fluoride, lead, mercury, nitrate, and radium to below baseline for the majority of well fields.

Analytes for which secondary standards have been established show that sulfate is the only constituent that increased in the majority of well fields after mining and remediation, whereas chloride, TDS, iron, and manganese decreased. Chemical constituents for which no MCL or secondary standards were set are higher than baseline for calcium, magnesium, bicarbonate, conductivity, alkalinity, and ammonia. Sodium, potassium, silica, and molybdenum were lower than baseline in the majority of well fields after mining and remediation.

For More Information Contact:

Susan Hall
U.S. Geological Survey
Central Energy Resources Science Center
Box 25046, MS 939
Denver, CO 80225

susanhall@usgs.gov
303-236-1656

References Cited

Energy Information Agency, 2009. EIA – Nuclear Data, Reports, Analysis, Surveys, 11 May 2009, accessed data at http://www.eia.doe.gov/fuelnuclear.html.

Long, P.E., Yabusaki, S.B., Meyer, P.D., Murray, C.J., N'Guessan, A.L., 2008, Technical basis for assessing uranium bioremediation performance: NUREG/CR-6973, U.S. Nuclear Regulatory Commission Office of Nuclear Research, 128 p.

LQD/DEQ Response Document, January 10, 2005 Comments, 2005, Irigaray Well field Restoration Report TFN 4 1/170 prepared by Cogema Mining Inc., Petrotek Engineering Corporation, and Resource Technologies Group.

Mays, W.M., 1994, Restoration of groundwater at three in-situ uranium mines in Texas, IAEA Technical Committee Meeting, Vienna Austria, Oct. 5-8, 1992 as reviewed in Nuexco Review, May 1994: Groundwater Restoration of In-Situ Uranium Mines.

Mobil, 1981, Internal company reports describing Mobil Oil Corporation's Crown Point ISR Pilot Test Project.

NDEQ, 2009, Nebraska Department of Environmental Quality Monthly Restoration Reports Crow Butte Mine Unit 4.

Nuclear Energy Agency, 2008, Uranium 2007 Resources, Production and Demand: a Joint Report by the OECD Nuclear Energy Agency and the International Atomic Energy Agency, 420 p.

Reimann, L. and Huffman, L., 2005, Biological reduction of metals during ground water restoration: presented at the Global Uranium Symposium, July 13, 2005, Casper, Wyoming.